Materiales cambiantes

Cambiar la forma

Chris Oxlade

Heinemann Library
Chicago, Illinois

www.heinemannraintree.com
Visit our website to find out more information about Heinemann-Raintree books.

To order:

☎ Phone 888-454-2279

💻 Visit www.heinemannraintree.com to browse our catalog and order online.

Edited by Charlotte Guillain and Rebecca Rissman
Designed by Ryan Frieson and Betsy Wernert
Translation into Spanish by DoubleO Publishing Services
Photo research by Elizabeth Alexander and Virginia Stroud-Lewis
Printed and bound by South China Printing Company Ltd.
Translation into Spanish by DoubleO Publishing Services

13 12 11 10
10 9 8 7 6 5 4 3 2 1

Library of Congress Cataloging-in-Publication Data
Oxlade, Chris.
 [Changing shape. English]
 Cambiar la forma / Chris Oxlade.
    p. cm.—(Materiales cambiantes)
 Includes bibliographical references and index.
 ISBN 978-1-4329-4428-5 (hc)—ISBN 978-1-4329-4433-9 (pb)
 1. Materials—Juvenile literature. 2. Materials—Mechanical properties—Juvenile literature. I. Title.
  TA403.2.O94818 2011
  620.1'1—dc22   2010004611

Acknowledgments

The author and publishers are grateful to the following for permission to reproduce copyright material: Alamy **pp. 6** (© Jorge Sanchez-Conejo), **9** (© Positive image), **13** (© Urban Zone), **21** (© David R. Frazier Photolibrary Inc.), **22** (© Chad Ehlers); Art Directors and Trip Photo Library **pp. 8, 12, 14, 15, 18, 23, 25** (Helene Rogers); © Capstone Global Library **pp. 4, 5, 16** (MM Studios); © Capstone Global Library Ltd. 2004 **p. 20** (Debbie Rowe); © Capstone Publishers **pp. 19, 26-29** (Karon Dubke); Photolibrary **pp. 10** (Digital Vision), **24** (© Odilon Dimier); Shutterstock **pp. 7** (© Stuart Miles), **11** (© Brian Chase).

Cover photograph of close-up of a woman holding colorful rubber bands reproduced with permission of Getty Images / © bilderlounge.

Every effort has been made to contact copyright holders of material reproduced in this book. Any omissions will be rectified in subsequent printings if notice is given to the publisher.

All the Internet addresses (URLs) given in this book were valid at the time of going to press. However, due to the dynamic nature of the Internet, some addresses may have changed, or sites may have changed or ceased to exist since publication. While the author and Publishers regret any inconvenience this may cause readers, no responsibility for any such changes can be accepted by either the author or the Publishers.

Contenido

Las palabras que aparecen en negrita, **como éstas**, se explican en el glosario.

Acerca de los materiales

¿Cuántos tipos diferentes de materiales conoces? ¿Ves algo de madera, de plástico o de metal en esta fotografía? Todos estos son materiales que usamos para fabricar cosas.

Estas cosas están hechas de materiales distintos.

¿Puedes ver un material natural y un material fabricado por seres humanos?

Algunos materiales son materiales **naturales**. Los obtenemos del mundo que nos rodea. La madera, la arcilla y el agua son materiales naturales. Los seres humanos fabrican otros materiales, como el vidrio y el plástico.

Materiales cambiantes

El hielo se convierte en agua cuando se derrite.

Los materiales pueden cambiar de forma.
A veces podemos cambiar las **propiedades** de
un material. Las propiedades de un material
incluyen cómo se ve y cómo se siente al tacto.

Podemos estirar o apretar algunos materiales para cambiar su forma. Algunos materiales cambian fácilmente de forma, como la plastilina.

La plastilina cambia de forma cuando la estiras.

Estirar

Cuando tiras de los extremos de un pedazo de material, se puede volver más largo. Los materiales cambian de forma cuando se estiran.

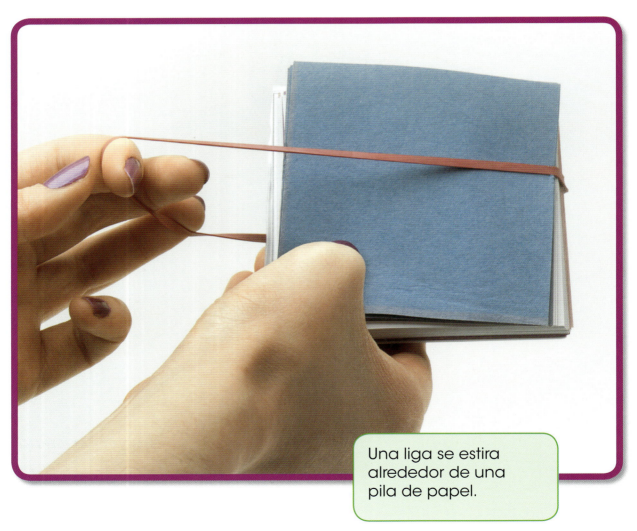

Una liga se estira alrededor de una pila de papel.

Algunos materiales son fáciles de estirar. Cuando los jalas se vuelven mucho más largos. También se vuelven más delgados cuando se estiran. Ciertos materiales, como las piedras, no se estiran fácilmente.

Un juguete de caucho se vuelve más largo y delgado cuando lo estiras.

Aplanar

Cuando aprietas los extremos de un pedazo de material, éste puede moverse. El material puede aplanarse. Aplanar es un cambio de forma.

Un juguete que rebota se aplana fácilmente.

La masa se vuelve más delgada y se expande cuando la aplanas con un rodillo.

Algunos materiales son fáciles de aplanar. Cuando los aplanas se vuelven más delgados. Ciertos materiales también se vuelven más cortos. Algunos materiales, como el vidrio, no se aplanan fácilmente.

Doblar y torcer

Esta regla de plástico cambia de forma cuando se dobla.

Cuando sostienes un objeto tomándolo por dos lugares y acercas tus manos, puedes hacer que el objeto se doble. Doblar un objeto puede hacer que cambie de forma.

Cuando enrollas la hélice de un avión a escala, tuerces la liga. La liga cambia de forma.

Los objetos **se tuercen** cuando giras sus extremos en direcciones opuestas. Torcer un objeto puede hacer que cambie de forma. No todos los materiales se doblan o se tuercen fácilmente.

Investigar cómo cambiar las formas

Trata de cambiar la forma de distintos materiales. Intenta estirarlos, aplanarlos, doblarlos y **torcerlos**. Aquí presentamos algunos materiales con los que puedes experimentar:

Materiales

Un pedazo delgado de madera

Una cuchara de plástico

Una taza de porcelana

Un pedazo de caucho

Plastilina

¿Es fácil doblar un palito de madera? ¿Cambia de forma?

¿Fue fácil o difícil cambiar la forma de los materiales con los que experimentaste? En un cuaderno, anota en una tabla las **propiedades** de cada material. Escribe el nombre del material en una columna y sus propiedades en la otra columna.

Material	Propiedades
Un pedazo de caucho	Se aplana, se dobla y se tuerce. Siempre vuelve a la misma forma.
Un pedazo delgado de madera	
Una cuchara de plástico	
Una taza de porcelana	
Plastilina	

Comparar materiales

En la página 14 **comparaste** la facilidad con la que se estiraban, se aplanaban, se doblaban y se **torcían** varios materiales. En la fotografía siguiente se ven algunos materiales con los que quizás hayas experimentado: piedra, vidrio, papel y cuero.

¿Puedes identificar los materiales que aparecen en esta fotografía?

La tabla siguiente muestra algunas **propiedades** de los materiales que aparecen en la fotografía anterior. ¿**Observaste** algunas de las mismas propiedades en tus experimentos?

Material	Propiedades
Piedra	No cambia de forma.
Vidrio	No cambia de forma.
Papel	No se estira. Se dobla y se tuerce fácilmente.
Cuero	Se estira un poco. Se dobla y se tuerce fácilmente. A veces recupera su forma original.

Materiales blandos y duros

Algunos materiales son blandos. Es fácil cambiar su forma. La plastilina es fácil de aplanar y de estirar porque es blanda. Puedes darle la forma que quieras.

Estos instrumentos hacen que la plastilina tome distintas formas.

Un cuchillo de metal corta porque es duro y no cambia de forma. Debes pedirle a un adulto que te ayude antes de usar un cuchillo.

Algunos materiales son duros. Es difícil cambiar su forma. Por ejemplo, es difícil aplanar una piedra.

Materiales flexibles

El papel es flexible. Puedes plegarlo para crear formas nuevas.

Algunos materiales son fáciles de doblar y de **torcer**. Usamos la palabra **flexible** para describir estos materiales.

Los pedazos delgados de un material son más fáciles de doblar que los pedazos gruesos del mismo material. Por ejemplo, puedes doblar fácilmente un clip de metal, pero no puedes doblar una barra gruesa de metal.

Las ramas delgadas de estos árboles se doblan con el viento, pero no las ramas gruesas.

Materiales rígidos y quebradizos

Es difícil hacer que algunos materiales cambien de forma. No se estiran, aplanan, doblan ni **tuercen**. Usamos el término tieso, o **rígido**, para describir estos materiales. La piedra y la porcelana son materiales duros y rígidos.

Los materiales rígidos como los ladrillos son buenos para la construcción.

Los palitos de pan no se doblan. Son quebradizos.

Si intentas cambiar la forma de ciertos materiales duros, el material puede romperse. Los materiales que se quiebran de esta manera se denominan materiales **quebradizos**.

Recuperar la forma

Un resorte de juguete siempre recupera su forma original.

Cuando estiras o aprietas un material para cambiar su forma y luego lo sueltas, a veces el material vuelve a su forma original. Por ejemplo, si aplanas una pelota de caucho, la pelota cambia de forma, pero recupera su forma original cuando la sueltas.

El alambre para jardinería conserva la forma que le das al doblarlo.

Si aprietas o estiras otros materiales, éstos conservan su nueva forma cuando los sueltas. Estos materiales son útiles para fabricar cosas. La plastilina conserva la forma que le das, para así hacer figuras.

Sólidos, líquidos y gases

Todos los materiales son **sólidos**, **líquidos** o **gases**. Por ejemplo, el hielo es un sólido, el agua es un líquido y el vapor es un gas. Los sólidos, los líquidos y los gases tienen **propiedades** diferentes.

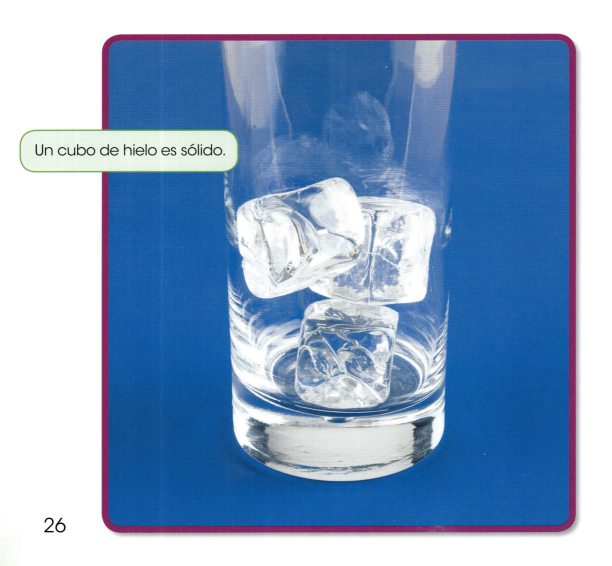

Un cubo de hielo es sólido.

Una bebida líquida cambia su forma para llenar el fondo de un vaso.

Un sólido conserva su forma a menos que algo lo haga cambiar. Los líquidos y los gases cambian más fácilmente de forma. Por ejemplo, un líquido siempre se extenderá para llenar un recipiente, y un gas como el aire llenará un globo por completo.

¿Cuál material?

Usamos materiales diferentes para cosas diferentes. Aquí se ven dos vasos. Uno está hecho de vidrio. El otro está hecho de papel. ¿Cuál le darías a un niño pequeño?

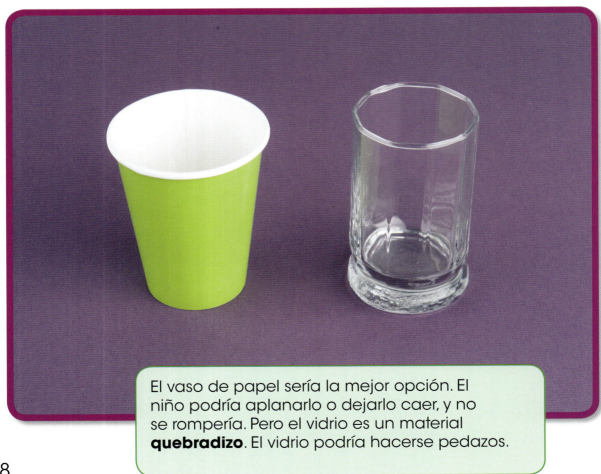

El vaso de papel sería la mejor opción. El niño podría aplanarlo o dejarlo caer, y no se rompería. Pero el vidrio es un material **quebradizo**. El vidrio podría hacerse pedazos.

Aquí se muestran dos cuchillos. Uno está hecho de plástico. El otro está hecho de metal. ¿Cuál es mejor para cortar un material como zanahorias crudas?

El cuchillo de metal sería mejor para cortar un material duro. El plástico cambia de forma más fácilmente. Se doblaría y **torcería** cuando intentaras cortar con él.

Glosario

comparar observar las diferencias entre dos o más cosas

flexible material que se dobla fácilmente

gas material que fluye y llena un espacio. El aire es un gas.

líquido material que fluye y llena el fondo de un recipiente. El agua es un líquido.

natural algo que no está hecho por las personas. Se obtiene de los animales, las plantas o las rocas de la Tierra.

observar mirar algo con atención

propiedad algo que nos indica cómo es un material; por ejemplo, cómo se ve o cómo se siente al tacto

quebradizo material que se rompe fácilmente cuando intentas doblarlo

rígido material que no se dobla ni se tuerce

sólido material que conserva la forma y no fluye. La madera es un sólido.

torcer apretar y tirar de los extremos de un objeto, haciendo que los extremos giren en direcciones opuestas

Aprende más

Libros

Bailey, Jacqui. *How Do We Use Materials?* Mankato, Minn.: Smart Apple Media, 2006.

Larousse México. *Materiales y materia (40 fantásticos experimentos)*. México: Larousse México, 2005.

Oxlade, Chris. *Using Materials* series (*Coal, Cotton, Glass, Metal, Oil, Paper, Plastic, Rock, Rubber, Silk, Soil, Water, Wood, Wool*). Chicago: Heinemann Library, 2004–2005.

Twist, Clint. *Materials*. New York: Bearport, 2006.

Sitios web

www.crickweb.co.uk/assets/resources/flash.
php?&file=materials

www.crickweb.co.uk/assets/resources/flash.
php?&file=materials2d

Visita estas páginas web para hallar actividades interactivas de ciencias.

Índice

CUSTOMS · COSTUMES AND CULTURES

FESTIVALS

by
Jerry Craven

Rourke Publications, Inc.
Vero Beach, Florida 32964

PHOTO CREDITS

Photophile
Picture Library Associates
Lauri Watanabe

Library of Congress Cataloging-in-Publication Data

Craven, Jerry.
    Festivals / Jerry Craven.
        p. cm. — (Customs, costumes, and cultures)
    Includes index.
    Summary: Introduces festivals celebrated in various places
throughout the world.
    ISBN 0-86625-594-X
    1. Festivals—Juvenile literature. [1. Festivals.] I. Title. II. Series.
GT3933.C73   1996
394.2'6—dc20   96-11395
                                                                    CIP
                                                                     AC

Printed in the U.S.A.

TABLE OF CONTENTS

CHAPTER 1
Festivals from Around the World

People living in the United States celebrate many **festival** (FES tuh vul) days. Americans look forward to these days so much that it is easy to believe the festivals started in the United States.

The truth is that many cultures have helped to make American festivals. Many different kinds of people have helped make festival foods, dances, and songs. Even the names of some festivals come from lands far away.

Festivals are important to people everywhere. The people in this parade live in Bali, a tiny island in the South Pacific. Every day of the year, people somewhere in Bali celebrate a festival of some kind.

One fun way to enjoy festivals is to put on special costumes. These children are dressed for a Japanese harvest festival.

A festival is one or more days set aside each year to remember special events or important ideas. All over the world people love festivals. They love to celebrate the coming of winter or the end of winter, the planting of crops or the harvesting of crops. They honor religious holidays and other special days. When people from around the world moved to the United States, they brought their festivals with them.

Even before they settled in America, their festivals were mixtures of many ancient cultures. From the Easter Bunny to Santa Claus, from giving valentines to wearing scary costumes on Halloween, the customs of festival days mix many cultures. American festivals are fun events that blend ideas from people of many religions and races.

CHAPTER 2
New Year's Day: January 1

Most people in the world agree that January 1 is the start of the new year. In the United States people celebrate the end of the old year on December 31 with a party. The high point of the party comes at midnight when the old year ends and the new one begins. Many cities have parades on January 1. In larger cities, the parades are broadcast on television.

About 2,150 years ago, the Romans set New Year's Day on January 1. January was named after Janus, the Roman god who had two faces, one on each side of his head. Janus could look forward into the new year and back into the last year.

Many people like to wear masks or paint their faces for parties on New Year's Eve.

There are, however, different kinds of calendars. Some people celebrate a different New Year's Day.

Fireworks are a traditional part of new year's celebrations in many countries.

The Chinese new year celebration begins in late January or early February and lasts one month. People in large Chinese communities the world over celebrate with lion dances and by setting off strings of firecrackers. The firecrackers are made from red paper because red is a lucky color. On some streets with lion dance parades, the people use so many firecrackers that dancers walk through red paper that is ankle deep.

This boy is wearing a mask designed for a New Year's Eve party.

The Jewish new year, called **Rosh Hashana** (RAHSH huh SHAH nuh), comes sometime between September 6 and October 5. The Rosh Hashana celebration lasts for two full days.

CHAPTER 3
Remember Your Valentine: An Ancient Custom

Millions of Americans send cards and flowers to friends on Valentine's Day. Not many people know Americans borrowed the holiday from another culture.

Over 2,000 years ago, the Romans celebrated a festival that later became St. Valentine's Day. Roman girls wrote love notes and signed them. They put these notes into a clay pot. Then boys drew the notes from the pot. They could date the girls whose names were on the notes. The Roman festival was called the **Lupercalia** (loo per KAY lee uh).

When Christianity came to Europe, Christians kept the holiday. They moved it a day earlier, to February 14, and changed its name. It became St. Valentine's Day in honor of a Roman named Valentine who died rather than give up his Christian beliefs.

This boy has just chosen flowers as a Valentine's Day gift for his family.

Many people like to add hearts and teddy bears to flowers on Valentine's Day.

One legend says that before his death, Valentine wrote a note to the young daughter of the jailer. She had become his friend, so he wrote to her, "Remember your Valentine."

The ancient Roman custom of boys drawing girls' names from pots continued for centuries. Today many people give cards to friends, both male and female.

Many people in the United States celebrate Valentine's Day by sending flowers to those they love. Roses are popular. People who work in flower shops say that Valentine's Day is one of the busiest days of the year.

CHAPTER 4
A Day to Wear Green: St. Patrick's Day

St. Patrick chased all the snakes out of Ireland, says the legend. Some Irish people believe the story. They point out that there are no native snakes in the entire island.

An important symbol of Ireland is the shamrock, or three-leaf clover. St. Patrick liked to use the shamrock as a symbol of Christianity. Today, people all over the United States know the shamrock stands for Ireland. Many people across the country like to wear something green to honor the Irish on March 17, which is St. Patrick's Day. They also send mail to two towns named "Shamrock," one in Texas and the other in Florida. The postal workers stamp the letters as if they were mailed in Shamrock, and send them on.

A PARADE OF IRISH PEOPLE

Some people like to joke that there are more Irish people in the New York St. Patrick's Day parade than there are in Ireland.

This man had a shamrock painted on his cheek before marching in a St. Patrick's Day parade in Atlanta, Georgia.

In Ireland, farmers celebrate St. Patrick's Day in two unusual ways. Many farmers choose the day to mark the end of winter. They put their cows and sheep out to pasture for the first time that year. Potato farmers like to plant potatoes on March 17.

In the United States, many cities have parades in honor of St. Patrick. The most famous St. Patrick's Day parades are in New York City, Atlanta, Boston, and Philadelphia.

CHAPTER 5
Easter Eggs, Bunnies, and Parades

Spring festivals celebrating the end of winter are important the world over. Most people celebrate a spring festival on the Sunday after the full moon in March. On that day in Japan, Buddhists celebrate both the coming of spring and the birthday of Buddha.

Easter is another spring festival. The English word for Easter came from *Eostre* or *Ostre*, the pagan goddess of the spring. Pagans believed there were many gods and goddesses. Christians borrowed the Easter Bunny and Easter eggs from pagan festivals.

The ancient tradition of coloring eggs came from pagans who gathered eggs of wild birds for the spring festival. The bunny, or hare, stood for the full moon. The full moon was important because it set the day of the festival. Christians today use eggs and the Easter Bunny as symbols of the Easter season.

Easter festivals in the United States include sunrise church services and parades. Most important to children, though, is the Easter egg hunt. In most houses, people color boiled eggs using a dye mixed with vinegar. Many small children believe the Easter Bunny hides the eggs for them to find.

WHEN IS EASTER?

The date of Easter depends upon the moon. Easter is the first Sunday after the full moon on or after March 21.

For most Americans, Easter would not be Easter without baskets of colored eggs.

In France, it is church bells that hide the eggs. Children believe the bells fly to Rome at night to get the eggs. Then the bells fly back and hide the eggs, just as the Easter Bunny does in other countries.

CHAPTER 6
A Festival for Fools

April Fools Day is a strange festival day in many ways. There are no special ceremonies. People do not dress up in special costumes. There are no traditional feast foods. What makes the day special is the many ways people pull jokes on each other.

People all over the world love a good joke. In almost every culture, there is a day set aside for pulling pranks. Today, that special day is April 1 in most parts of the world.

SOME POPULAR APRIL FOOL TRICKS ARE:

1. Gluing a coin to the sidewalk and watching people try to pick it up.

2. Cooking a piece of white cloth into a pancake so it is impossible to cut or bite.

3. Leaving someone a telephone number and a message to call and ask for "Mr. Seal" or "Miss Lion," or some other animal's name. The phone number is the one for the local zoo. This trick happens so often in America that many zoos disconnect their phones on April 1.

4. Tying a $10 bill to a string and leaving the bill on a sidewalk. When someone tries to pick up the bill, the trickster jerks it away with the string.

Three people distract a friend while one of them puts an April Fools' fish on her back. In the background is a person who has already been tricked.

In France, April 1 is called "fish day." The French like to sneak up to their friends and tape paper fish on their backs. The fun is watching them go out in public without knowing about the fish they have on their backs.

CHAPTER 7
Ramadan: A Time for Fasting

Once each year people of the Islamic, or **Muslim** (MUZ lum), religion do not eat or drink anything during daylight hours for an entire month. This is the month named **Ramadan** (RAH muh dahn) in the Muslim calendar. At the end of each day's fast, many Muslims celebrate with a feast.

The time when Ramadan begins changes each year. The Muslim calendar is different from the one most people use. Because Muslims measure a year by the changes in the moon, their year has 355 days. Most people measure a year by the

This is the Great Blue Mosque in Malaysia, a popular place of worship during Ramadan.

This is one of the largest mosques in Borneo, where Muslim people in the city of Kuching worship, especially during the Ramadan festival.

number of days it takes for the Earth to go around the sun. That number is 365 days and six hours. A Muslim year is shorter by 10 days. This is why Ramadan comes earlier each year, as most people measure a year.

Ramadan is a holy month for Muslims. It is a time to be grateful to God for the gift of their holy book, The **Koran** (kuh RAN). Most Muslims enjoy wonderful foods as soon as the sun sets. Some Muslim people prepare food during the day, then eat several festive meals during the night. However, people who are ill don't have to fast during the day.

In ancient times most people did not have clocks. Muslims judged the end of day by looking at a white thread hanging next to a black thread. When they could not tell the difference between the two, night began and they could eat and drink. Then they used the same test to find out when to start fasting in the morning. When they could see which thread was white, the fast began again.

CHAPTER 8
Ghosts and Games on Halloween

Long ago, October 31 marked the end of the year. That day became a festival day for two reasons. One was to welcome the new year and the winter season. The other was to say goodbye to the old year and to honor those who had died.

Some people feared the ghosts of the dead. They hollowed out turnips and pumpkins to make them into lanterns. People believed that lanterns hanging in a window or a doorway kept ghosts out of the house.

Many people still put jack-o-lanterns such as this one in their windows on Halloween night.

Out trick-or-treating, this girl carries a jack-o-lantern as part of her costume.

One folk story tells about how Irish Jack couldn't get into heaven because he was too mean. He didn't fit well in the Devil's kingdom, either. Satan kicked him out for playing too many tricks. On Halloween, he walked on the Earth, playing mean tricks on people. People figured out that Irish Jack was afraid of pumpkin and turnip lanterns, so they kept them burning all night long on Halloween. They called the special lights "Jack-o-lanterns."

In Ireland, people built bonfires on Halloween to scare away ghosts. They also played games around the fire, just as many people do today. One game was to throw nuts into the fire. If the nuts exploded in flame, it meant the person who tossed them would have an unhappy marriage.

CHAPTER 9
Chocolate Coffins and Sugar Skulls: Celebrating the Day of the Dead

For many Americans, November 2 is a day to go to a cemetery for a picnic.

Latino Americans call it *Día de los Muertos* (DEE uh day los MWER tohs), or the "Day of the Dead." In Mexico, it is a national holiday.

The Day of the Dead is a festival for remembering friends and relatives who have died. It begins as a family affair at home. In some cities there is a parade to the cemetery where people share a picnic lunch.

On the Day of the Dead, many people dress in costumes that look like those of Halloween. No one tries to be scary, though. These people use their costumes to call attention to the changes that death brings.

On the oferenda, *people place flowers, models of skulls, and favorite foods of dead relatives.*

Some believe the dead return in spirit for the festival. Relatives prepare the favorite foods once enjoyed by those they have lost. This food goes on a special table in the home, called the *oferenda* (oh fer END uh). They do not believe the ghosts return to eat the food. People put out the food as a way of remembering those who have died.

In Sacramento, California, as in many other American cities, preparations for the festival begin in late October. Family members bend a piece of cane into an arch, then decorate the arch with flowers and ribbons. The arch goes over the oferenda, which the family also decorates.

Many families in San Antonio, Texas, cook meals in the cemetery. A traditional food is *pan de muertos* (PAHN day MWER tohs), or "bread of the dead." This is bread baked in the shape of skulls or bodies. Children eat chocolate candy shaped like coffins or skulls, and sugar candy shaped like hearses and funeral wreaths.

While the festival is fun, it is also a serious day for mourning those who have died.

CHAPTER 10
Celebrating the Harvest: The Thanksgiving Festival

In many countries winter can be long and cold. People must store food for the months of ice and snow. Just before winter, they harvest crops. Then they have a thanksgiving festival to celebrate the harvest.

The first Thanksgiving Day in America was a harvest festival. In 1621, Governor Bradford of Plymouth Colony said it was time to celebrate the harvest. It wasn't a big harvest, but the people were grateful for it. They invited their neighbors, a tribe of Native Americans led by Chief Massasoit.

The Native Americans brought five deer to share at the feast. The colonists cooked the deer, along with many wild turkeys. They also cooked corn cakes and cranberries. People ate outdoors.

THANK OUR PRESIDENTS FOR THANKSGIVING

Two American presidents were important in the history of Thanksgiving Day.

- George Washington asked the United States to celebrate its first national Thanksgiving Day on November 26, 1789.

- In 1863, Abraham Lincoln made Thanksgiving a national holiday to be celebrated each year.

Since the first Thanksgiving in the year 1621, turkey has been a favorite part of the festival meal.

Chief Massasoit and 90 Native Americans came to the festival and stayed for three days. People spent most of the first day eating. On the second and third days, they danced, ran races, and held wrestling contests.

Harvest festivals were more important in the past than they are today. Before people invented canning or refrigeration, long winters often meant running out of food. A harvest feast was usually the last big meal people ate before winter began.

Today, Americans still celebrate Thanksgiving Day by eating a special meal. They eat food similar to what the Colonists shared with Native Americans during the first Thanksgiving feast.

CHAPTER 11
The Festival of Lights: Eight Days of Gifts and Games

Hanukkah (HAH nuh kuh) is a festival celebrating the survival of Judaism. Hanukkah is sometimes spelled *Chanukah.* The Hanukkah festival occurs close to the time of Christmas. Jewish families decorate their houses for Hanukkah much as Christians do for Christmas. During Hanukkah, children get gifts and play games with all members of the family.

Most Jewish families have a special Hanukkah candle holder, called a menorah, *like the one this girl is lighting.*

Hanukkah is a time for families to be together and celebrate the survival of their religion.

Hanukkah is called "The Festival of Lights" because people use candles each day of the festival. On the first night of Hanukkah, each family lights a candle. It sits in a special candle holder called a **menorah** (muh NOR uh). The menorah holds nine candles—one for each of the eight days of the festival plus a **shammash** (SHAH mus). This is a candle used to light the others. On the second night, the family lights two candles, and on the third night, three. On the eighth night, the family lights all the candles in the menorah.

The festival is also called "days of dedication." Over 2,000 years ago, the Hebrew army defeated the army of a Syrian king. The Hebrews took over Jerusalem and made a building used by Muslims into a Jewish temple. The story says that in the temple there was an oil lamp with enough oil to burn only one day. Somehow the lamp burned for eight days. Burning eight candles during Hanukkah is a way of remembering an ancient victory.

CHAPTER 12
The Many Faces of Santa Claus

Why is Santa Claus a part of Christmas? Christmas celebrates the birthday of Jesus, and he was born in a land where it never snows. However, Santa lives at the North Pole, wears a warm red coat trimmed in fur, and he comes down chimneys.

People told stories about Santa before the beginning of the United States. The story that he rides a snow sled pulled by reindeer came from cold countries in northern Europe. Everywhere Santa is a gift-giver who brings toys to children. However, he looks different to people of different cultures. He also has different names.

From left to right, these Santas are Irish, English, and Norwegian.

These Santa figures are, from the left, Russian, American frontier, and Scottish. The Scottish Santa is called "The Abbot of Unreason."

In Sweden, Santa is Father Christmas. He drives a sled pulled by goats. The Swedish Santa is based on a Nordic sky god named Thor. The idea that Santa Claus comes down chimneys comes from the story of Hertha, a Norse goddess. Hertha stepped out of the fireplace in the middle of the winter to give gifts to children.

In Italy, Santa is a woman named **Befana** (be FAHN ah). She rides a broomstick to children's homes. Good children get gifts. For bad ones, Befana leaves soot and ashes.

In France, people call Santa "Father Noel." Some people in Scotland call him "The Abbot of Unreason." No matter what people call him, he brings gifts to children on Christmas.

CHAPTER 13
Kwanzaa, a New Festival

Over 10 million African Americans now celebrate a week-long festival called **Kwanzaa** (KWAHN zuh). It is a new festival, compared to most others. Dr. Maulana Karenga thought of Kwanzaa in 1966. He was a teacher of African-American Studies in a California university. Dr. Karenga described ways to celebrate Kwanzaa that many people still follow today.

The word *kwanzaa* comes from an African language called Swahili. The word means "first fruits of harvest." The American festivities are based on an African harvest festival. In some ways the celebration is like Christmas. In others ways Kwanzaa is like Hanukkah.

During the week of Kwanzaa, family members and friends exchange gifts. Many think the gifts should be handmade and celebrate African-American culture. The festival begins on December 26 with lighting one candle in a group of seven. The candles are red, green, and black. In each of the following nights, family members light another candle.

Every night of the festival, family and friends talk about a different way to help people in the African-American community.

A writer named Cedric McClester created Nia Umoja. Nia Umoja is a bearded African American who is a symbol of Kwanzaa. The words *nia umoja* come from Swahili. They mean "purpose and unity." Nia Umoja is a teller of stories about how African Americans live and work together.

People celebrate the Kwanzaa festival by wearing traditional African costumes like this one.

CHAPTER 14
The Love of Festivals

People in the United States celebrate many festival days. A favorite one is Independence Day, or the Fourth of July. On this day, people celebrate the birthday of the country. It was on July 4 in 1776 that the people in the United States decided they would no longer be ruled by England.

On Mother's Day (the second Sunday in May), people honor their mothers. A similar festival is Father's Day, on the third Sunday in June. Other important holidays are Lincoln's birthday, February 12, and Flag Day, June 14.

Some states have their own special holidays. People in New Hampshire celebrate Fast Day. Fast Day, the fourth Monday in April, is a day for celebrating the end of winter and the beginning of spring planting.

Some cities even have festivals of their own. In the south Texas city Corpus Christi, for example, people have a parade on Buccaneer's Day. Most children dress up like pirates. People in other Texas cities don't celebrate Buccaneer's Day.

People the world over love festival days. There are so many that a list of them would fill a book larger than a dictionary.

Because Independence Day comes when the first melons of the season are ripe, watermelon has become a popular treat for July Fourth festivals.

GLOSSARY

Befana (be FAHN uh) – a woman who acts like Santa Claus. She brings Christmas toys to children in Italy.

Día de los Muertos (DEE uh day los MWER tohs) – a Spanish term meaning the "Day of the Dead." It is a festival on November 2 to honor friends and relatives who have died. The day is important to many Latino people.

festival (FES tuh vul) – one or more days set aside each year to remember special events or ideas.

Hanukkah (HAH nuh kuh) – also spelled *Chanukah*, the Festival of Lights, an important eight-day celebration for Hebrew people.

The Koran (kuh RAN) – the holy book of the Muslim people.

Kwanzaa (KWAHN zuh) – a week-long festival to honor the traditions of African-American people. It was first celebrated in 1966.

Lupercalia (loo pur KAY lee uh) – an ancient Roman festival that became Valentine's Day.

menorah (muh NOR uh) – a candle holder for the candles used by Jewish families during Hanukkah.

Muslim (MUZ lum) – a person who believes the Islamic religion. The Arabic meaning of the word is "one who surrenders to God."

oferenda (oh fer END uh) – a Spanish word meaning "gift" or "offering." It is a special table set up to hold food and other items important in the Day of the Dead festival.

pan de muertos (PAHN day MWER tohs) – a Spanish term meaning "bread of the dead." It is a special bread baked during the Day of the Dead festival.

Ramadan (RAH muh dahn) – a month-long festival among people of the Islamic religion. During this month, Muslims do not eat or drink anything during the daylight hours.

Rosh Hashana – (RAHSH huh SHAH nuh) – the Jewish new year.

shammash (SHAH mus) – a candle used to light other candles during the Festival of Lights.

INDEX